JUST BRASS

directed by

Philip Jones and Elgar Howarth

TUBA SOLOS
VOLUME ONE

arranged and edited by

JOHN FLETCHER

CONTENTS

		Score	Part
1. The Policeman's Song	Sullivan	1	2
2. Sanctus	Berlioz	3	3
3. When Britain really ruled the waves	Sullivan	5	4
4. Der Lindenbaum	Schubert	6	4
5. Hey-ho, come to the Fair	Martin	11	6
6. Oh, is there not one maiden breast?	Sullivan	14	7
7. Variations on a Temperance Theme	Parkhurst	16	8

This volume is available in versions for Tuba in C, E♭ Bass and BB♭ Bass

> WARNING: the photocopying of any pages of this publication is illegal. If copies are made in breach of copyright, the Publishers will, where possible, sue for damages.
>
> Every illegal copy means a lost sale. Lost sales lead to to shorter print runs and rising prices. Soon the music goes out of print, and more fine works are lost from the repertoire.

CHESTER MUSIC LIMITED

(A division of Music Sales Limited)

8/9 Frith Street, London W1V 5TZ.

TUBA SOLOS

arranged and edited by
John Fletcher

1.
THE POLICEMAN'S SONG

from *The Pirates of Penzance*

Arthur Sullivan

* Play only if the tuba needs to rest here.

© Copyright for all Countries 1982
J & W Chester/Edition Wilhelm Hansen London Ltd

CH55458

All rights reserved
Printed in England

2.
SANCTUS
from *Grande Messe des Morts*

Hector Berlioz

3.
WHEN BRITAIN REALLY RULED THE WAVES

from *Iolanthe*

Arthur Sullivan

4.
DER LINDENBAUM
(The Linden Tree)

Franz Schubert

5.
HEY-HO, COME TO THE FAIR
(But Don't Be Silly)

Easthope Martin

6.
OH, IS THERE NOT ONE MAIDEN BREAST?

from *The Pirates of Penzance*

Arthur Sullivan

7.
VARIATIONS ON A TEMPERANCE THEME

(Father's a drunkard and Mother is dead)

Mrs. E.A. Parkhurst

VARIATION I

Waltz time [♩ = 120]

VARIATION II

JUNIOR JUST BRASS

directed by Philip Jones & Elgar Howarth

An exciting new series from Chester Music which provides interesting and flexible ensemble music for less experienced players. Most of the works in the series will be in 4 or 5 versatile parts with optional percussion where suitable.

This blend of arrangements and original pieces so far includes:

1 JJB **SUITE** Elgar Howarth
2 tpts, hn, tbn

2 JJB **THREE LITTLE SUITES** Peter Lawrence
2 tpts, hn, 2 tbns

3 JJB **FOUR CAROLS** arr. Rory Boyle
2 tpts, hn, tbn, bass tbn/tuba, perc

4 JJB **MORE CAROLS** arr. Rory Boyle
2 tpts, hn, tbn, bass tbn/tuba, perc

5 JJB **SEVEN MOODS AND DANCES** Stephan de Haan
2 tpts, hn, tbn, perc

6 JJB **POPS FOR FOUR** Chris Hazell
2 tpts, hn, tbn, perc

7 JJB **THREE NORWEGIAN TUNES** Grieg, arr. Peter Reeve
2 tpts, hn, tbn, bass tbn/tuba, perc

8 JJB **THREE MINIATURES** Ian MacDonald
2 tpts, hn, tbn, bass tbn/tuba

9 JJB **MISCELLANY ONE** David S. Morgan
2 tpts, hn, tbn

10 JJB **THREE LATIN AMERICAN DANCES** Bruce Fraser
2 tpts, hn, tbn, perc

11 JJB **BASED ON THE BLUES** Dave Perrotet
2 tpts, hn, tbn, bass tbn/tuba

12 JJB **FOUR DANCES FROM TERPSICHORE** Michael Praetorius, arr. Peter Reeve
2 tpts, hn, tbn, bass tbn/tuba

13 JJB **THREE SEA SHANTIES** arr. Colin A. H. Asher
2 tpts, hn, tbn

14 JJB **FIVE BAGATELLES** Gordon Jacob
2 tpts, hn, tbn

15 JJB **AMERICANA** Harold East
2 tpts, hn, tbn

16 JJB **FOUR SPIRITUALS** arr. Colin A. H. Asher
2 tpts, hn, tbn

17 JJB **THREE HUNGARIAN FOLKSONGS** arr. Eric Crees
2 tpts, hn, tbn, perc

18 JJB **POMP AND CIRCUMSTANCE** (two famous themes) Elgar arr. Roger Harvey
2 tpts, hn, tbn, bass tbn/tuba

19 JJB **MISCELLANY TWO** David S. Morgan
2 tpts, hn, tbn

Substitute trombone parts are provided to cover the horn parts, and parts for E♭ horn, E♭ bass and BB♭ bass are included wherever practicable. Trombone parts are always provided in both treble and bass clefs.

More details from:

CHESTER MUSIC LIMITED
(a division of Music Sales Limited)
8/9 Frith Street, London. W1V 5TZ

Exclusive distributors:
MUSIC SALES LIMITED,
Newmarket Road, Bury St. Edmunds,
Suffolk. IP33 3YB